Read All About
Earthly Oddities

LIGHTS IN
THE SKY

Patricia Armentrout

The Rourke Press, Inc.
Vero Beach, Florida 32964

PHOTO CREDITS
© Alaska Division of Tourism: pg. 19; © Dick Dietrich: Cover, pgs. 9, 13, 22; © East Coast Studios: pg. 12; © Finley Holiday Films: pgs. 15, 16; © NASA: pgs. 4, 6, 21; © David E. Rogers: pg. 7; © James P. Rowan: pg. 10; © Yutaka Suzuki/Alaska Division of Tourism: pg. 18

ACKNOWLEDGMENTS
The author wishes to acknowledge David Armentrout for his contribution in writing this book.

Library of Congress Cataloging-in-Publication Data

Armentrout, Patricia, 1960-
    Lights in the sky / by Patricia Armentrout.
        p. cm. — (Earthly Oddities)
    Includes index.
    Summary: Describes various kinds of lights seen in the sky including rainbows, lightning, and the aurora borealis.
    ISBN 1-57103-155-3
    1. Atmospheric electricity—Juvenile literature.   2. Lightning—Juvenile literature.   3. Rainbow—Juvenile literature.
[1. Lightning.   2. Rainbow.]
I. Title II. Series: Armentrout, Patricia, 1960- Earthly Oddities.
QC966.5.A76 1996
551.5'6—dc20   96–2881
                                                              CIP
                                                               AC

Printed in the USA

TABLE OF CONTENTS

LIGHTNING

Cumulonimbus (kyoom yuh lo NIM bus) clouds produce thunderstorms. Thunderstorms make lightning and thunder.

Inside thunderstorms is a buildup of energy called charges. Positive and negative charges attract each other. When these opposite charges meet, they cause lightning. The gases in the air around lightning expand quickly and violently, producing thunder.

The amount of electricity in lightning is dangerous, and the heat is extreme. The air around a lightning strike is five times hotter than the surface of the sun!

This picture of thunderstorms forming over the Pacific Ocean was taken by astronauts aboard the space shuttle Discovery.

LIGHTNING STRIKES!

Lightning often strikes metal objects like power stations. It also strikes buildings, planes, and people. Lightning kills about a hundred people each year in the United States.

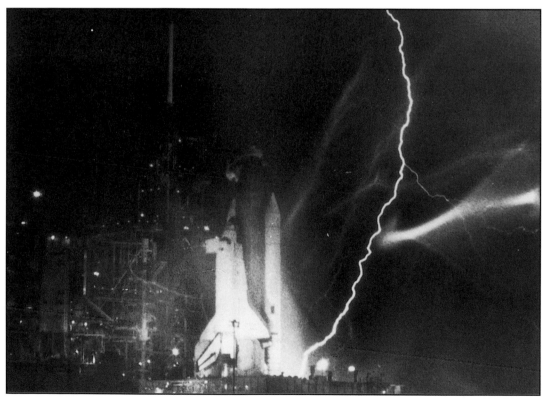

NASA must cancel launches when thunderstorms are in the area.

This bolt of lightning seems to be striking from the edge of the cloud formation.

You can judge the distance of a lightning strike using this simple rule: After seeing a lightning flash, count the number of seconds it takes to hear the thunder. Five seconds equals one mile. If you are able to count to five before you hear the thunder, you know the storm is one mile away. After several tests, if the number of seconds decreases, you know the thunderstorm is moving in your direction.

RAINBOWS

One of Earth's most beautiful oddities is the rainbow. A rainbow is probably the best part of a rainstorm. What is it about a rainbow? The colors!

A single rainbow, from top to bottom, shows red, orange, yellow, green, blue, and violet. If you happen to see a double rainbow, the band of colors on the top rainbow will show the same colors in reverse order.

The sky around this colorful rainbow still shows signs of a stormy day.

RAINBOW SHAPES

Rainbows are usually seen as an arc, or half circle, in the sky. But all rainbows are full circles. A full-circle rainbow cannot be seen from the ground, but one can be viewed from an airplane.

Rainbows show the colors of sunlight. To see a rainbow, you must have the sun to your back and raindrops in front of you. The sun shines through water droplets and comes out the other side as colors in the sky. How bright the colors appear depends on the angle of the sunlight shining through the water.

Rainbows are often seen near Niagara Falls because of the constant mist in the air.

MAKING A RAINBOW

We know it takes water and light to make a rainbow, but you don't have to wait for a rainstorm to see one. Try this: Stand outside with your back towards the afternoon sun. Now turn on a garden hose to a fine spray. Look through the spray, and you should be able to see a rainbow.

A fine spray of water and the sun to your back can help you make a rainbow.

A double rainbow appears over the Grand Canyon after a summer storm.

Have a friend look for a rainbow too. The rainbow he or she sees will be different from the one you see, even if the two of you are standing side by side. You are viewing the rainbow through different water droplets than your friend.

STARS

Did you know that the sun is a star? It is a huge ball of hot gas just like all other stars. Our star system, called the Milky Way, contains more than 100 billion stars.

The sun is our closest star, but it is over ninety-two million miles from Earth. The huge glowing ball of gas has a surface temperature of 6,000 degrees.

When we look into the night sky and see stars, we can make out patterns called **constellations** (KAHN stuh LAY shunz). Some well-known patterns are the Big and Little Dipper, Orion, and the Northern Cross.

The sun, our closest star, is a huge ball of hot gas.

COMETS

A comet is made of ice, gases, grit, and dust. Comets orbit, or move in a path around, the sun like the planets in our solar system.

Comets absorb light from the sun and then shine on their own. The brightness of the light depends on how close the comet is to the sun.

When a comet moves past the sun, it collects small bits of gas that mixes with its own gases. The gases give off light in the form of a tail.

A comet's tail can reach lengths of up to 60 million miles.

NORTHERN LIGHTS

Northern lights are beautiful displays of light in the sky. Northern lights, or **aurora borealis** (aw RAWR uh) (bawr ee AL is), have been occurring in the upper **atmosphere** (AT muh SFEER) for thousands of years. You may not have seen or heard of auroras, because they appear in places where very few people live.

Auroras have been occurring for thousand of years, yet very few people have seen them.

Aurora displays are best seen in the dark, late hours of the night.

Northern lights are seen in places close to the North Pole, such as areas of Canada and Alaska. Southern lights appear in the same way around the South Pole. Scientists call southern lights **aurora australis** (aw RAWR uh) (aw STRAY lis).

AURORA CAUSES

Why do auroras appear high overhead? The sun is constantly sending energy towards the Earth. Around Earth is its own energy, called a magnetic field. The two forces collide, or meet, with gases in the upper atmosphere and cause the auroras.

The lights can only be seen in the dark, even though they occur 24 hours a day. During an aurora display, color can sway gently or sometimes move unevenly. The colors and movements depend on the amount of energy and gases in the air.

The crew of the space shuttle Endeavor saw the Southern lights several times during this flight.

GLOSSARY

atmosphere (AT muh SFEER) — the air surrounding Earth

aurora australis (aw RAWR uh) (aw STRAY lis) — lights in the night sky that usually can be seen only around the South Pole

aurora borealis (aw RAWR uh) (bawr ee AL is) — lights in the night sky that usually can be seen only around the North Pole

constellations (KAHN stuh LAY shunz) — groups of stars that form patterns

cumulonimbus (kyoom yuh lo NIM bus) — clouds that cause thunderstorms

One of Earth's most beautiful oddities is the rainbow.

INDEX